It's Catching

Colds and Flu

Angela Royston

Heinemann
LIBRARY

www.heinemann.co.uk
Visit our website to find out more information about **Heinemann Library** books.

To order:

 Phone 44 (0) 1865 888066

Send a fax to 44 (0) 1865 314091

 Visit the Heinemann Bookshop at www.heinemann.co.uk to browse our catalogue and order online.

First published in Great Britain by Heinemann Library,
Halley Court, Jordan Hill, Oxford OX2 8EJ
a division of Reed Educational and Professional Publishing Ltd.
Heinemann is a registered trademark of Reed Educational & Professional Publishing Ltd.

OXFORD MELBOURNE AUCKLAND JOHANNESBURG BLANTYRE
GABORONE IBADAN PORTSMOUTH (NH) USA CHICAGO

Designed by David Oakley/Arnos Design
Illustrations by Jeff Edwards
Originated by Dot Gradations
Printed in Hong Kong/China

ISBN 0 431 12851 0
05 04 03 02 01
10 9 8 7 6 5 4 3 2 1

British Library Cataloguing in Publication Data
Royston, Angela
    Colds and flu. – (It's catching)
    1. Influenza 2. Cold (Disease)
    I. Title
    616.2'03

Acknowledgements
The publishers would like to thank the following for permission to reproduce photographs:
Bubbles (Claire Paxton) p26, Gareth Boden pp4, 5, 28, 29, PhotoDisc (Ryan McVay) p10, Science Photo Library pp7 (P Motta), 8 (Linda Stannard), 9 (Linda Stannard), 11 (Oscar Burriel), 13, 14 (Omikron), 15 (Gable Jerrican), 17 (Galliard Jerrican), 18 (John Greim), 21 (Sheila Terry), 23 (Brian Yarvin), 24, 25 (Geoff Tompkinson), Stone (Ben Edwards) p22, Tony Stone pp12 (Suzanne and Nick Geary), 16 (Vincent Oliver), 19 (Elie Bernager), 27 (Andy Sacks).

Cover photograph reproduced with permission of Stone (James Darell).

Any words appearing in bold, **like this**, are explained in the glossary.

Contents

What are colds and flu?

Colds and **flu** are two different illnesses.
Both of them affect your nose, **throat**
and breathing tubes.

Colds and flu are very **infectious**. This means that they are passed very easily from one person to another.

Healthy nose and throat

You take air into your body through your nose and mouth. The air passes down your **throat** into your breathing tubes and then into your **lungs**.

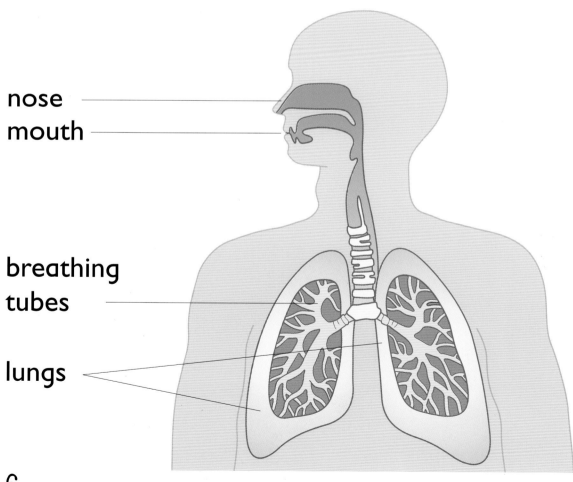

nose

mouth

breathing tubes

lungs

Tiny hairs in the nose and tubes help to catch dirt and **germs** before they reach your lungs. This is what the hairs look like under a **microscope**.

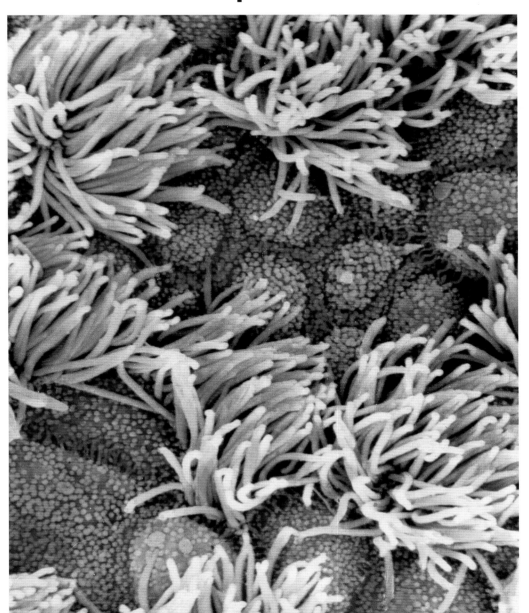

What causes colds and flu?

Colds and **flu** are caused by tiny germs called **viruses**. There are several different viruses that cause colds and others that cause flu.

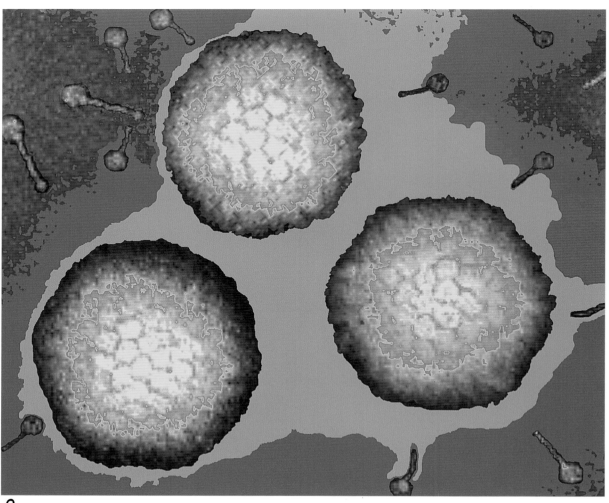

The pictures show two of the viruses through a **microscope**. They have been specially coloured to show them more clearly.

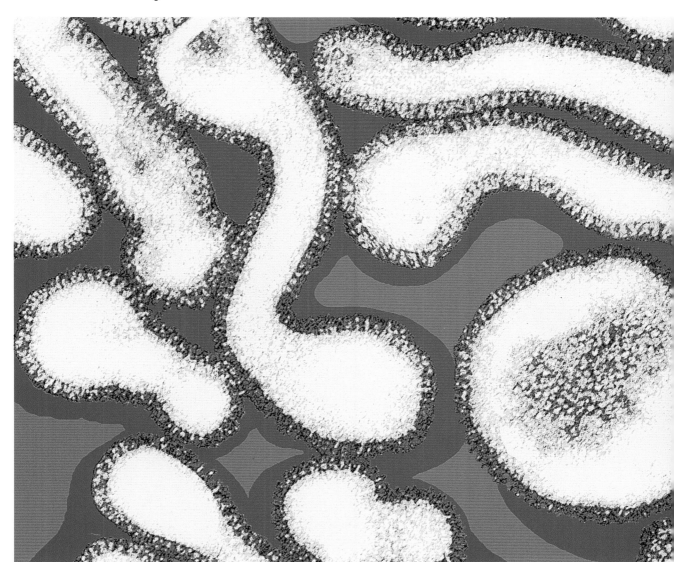

How do you catch a cold?

Every time someone with a **cold** or **flu** breathes out, lots of tiny **germs** are carried into the air. Anyone nearby will breathe in some of the germs.

The germs may make them ill, too. Coughing or sneezing pushes out many more germs — millions of germs every time!

First signs

The first sign that you have a **cold** could be sneezing, a sore **throat**, or a headache. It could be all three of these!

When you catch **flu**, you will probably feel very miserable. You may also feel shivery and your **muscles** and **joints** may ache.

What happens next?

Cold and **flu viruses** attack the nose, **throat** and breathing tubes. Special **blood cells** (like the one coloured green in the photo) kill the viruses.

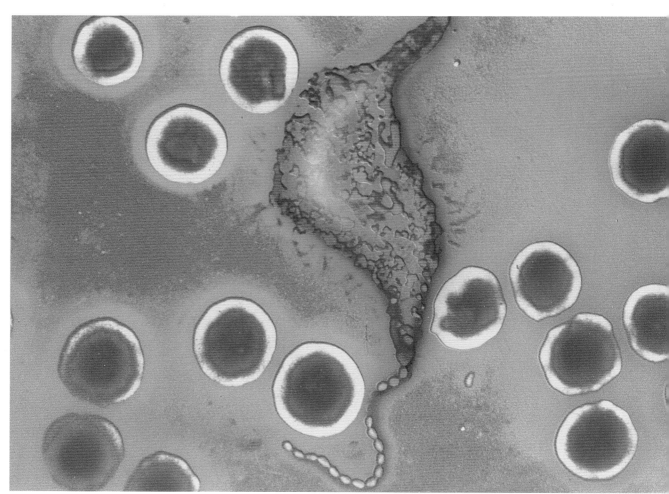

Your body also makes lots of **mucus** to wash away the viruses. Too much mucus can block your nose or make your nose runny.

Flu

When your body fights a **flu virus**, your **blood** becomes hotter. This is called a **fever**. A high fever can make you feel very ill.

You may feel cold but your whole body is hotter than normal. A **thermometer** can be used to measure your **temperature.**

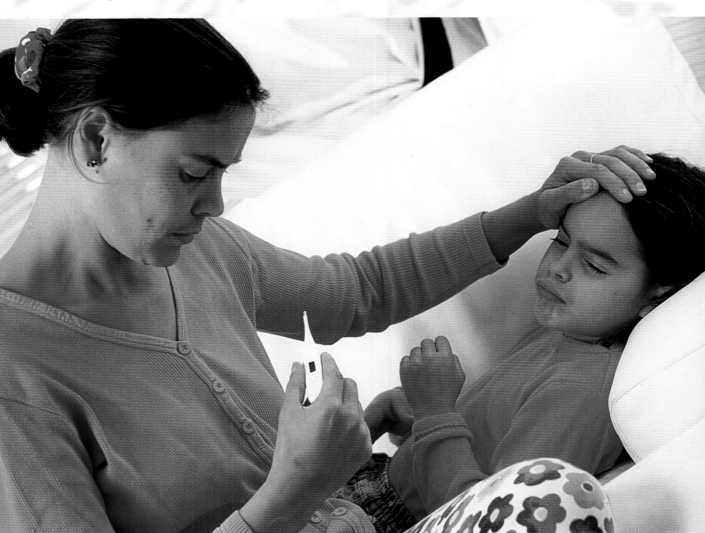

Treatment

There is no **medicine** that will make your **cold** or **flu** go away more quickly. If you are given a **painkiller** though, it will help you feel less ill.

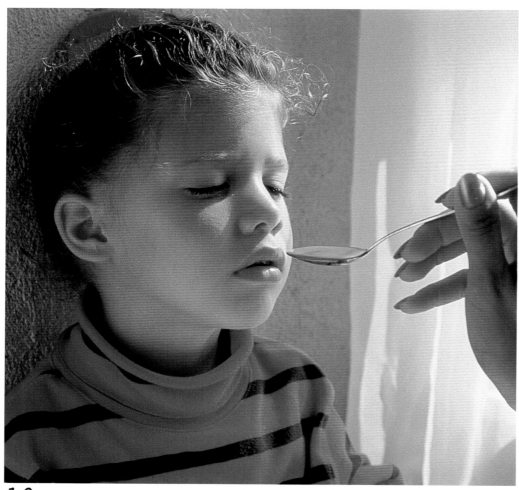

Painkillers help you feel more comfortable, but you should never be given more than the bottle says. Plenty of rest and cool drinks will help too.

Coughs

After seven to ten days you should feel much better. Even when you feel better, the tubes in your chest may still be full of **mucus**.

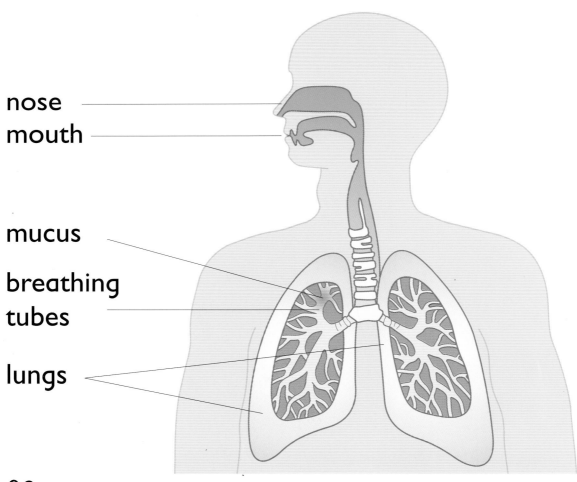

nose

mouth

mucus

breathing tubes

lungs

Coughing helps clear away extra mucus left in your chest. If the cough stops you sleeping, you can take some cough **medicine** to soothe it.

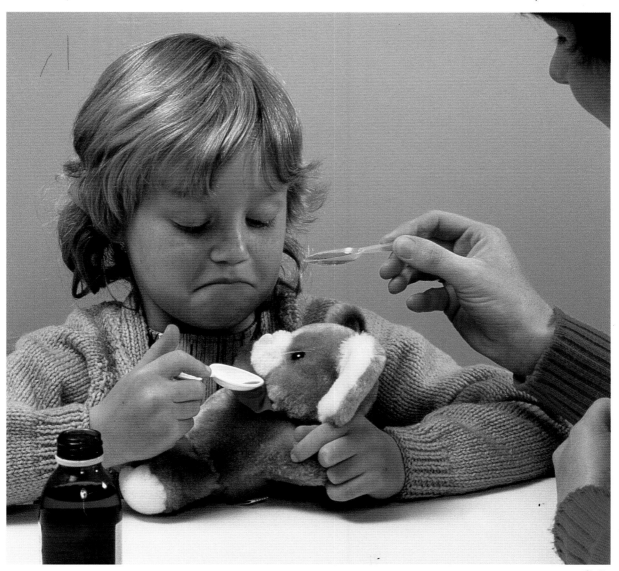

Another illness

Sometimes a **cold** or **flu** can lead to another, different illness. If you start coughing up green **mucus**, you may have a chest **infection**.

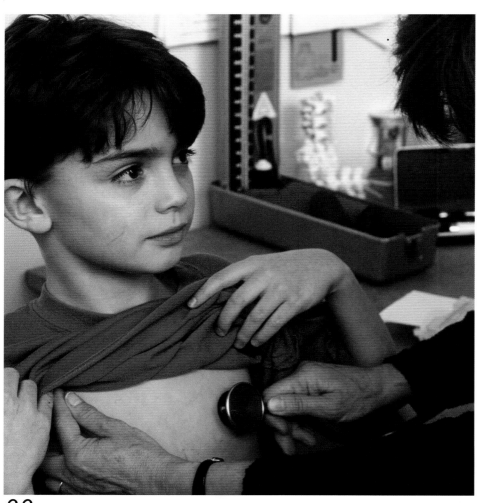

If you get bad earache, you may have an ear infection. A doctor can give you some **medicine** to make your ear or chest better.

Looking for a cure

Scientists try to find cures for **colds** and **flu**. This is very difficult because there are so many different **viruses** – and new ones keep appearing!

Some people have a flu **injection** each winter. The injection helps them to fight the most common flu viruses, so that they do not get ill.

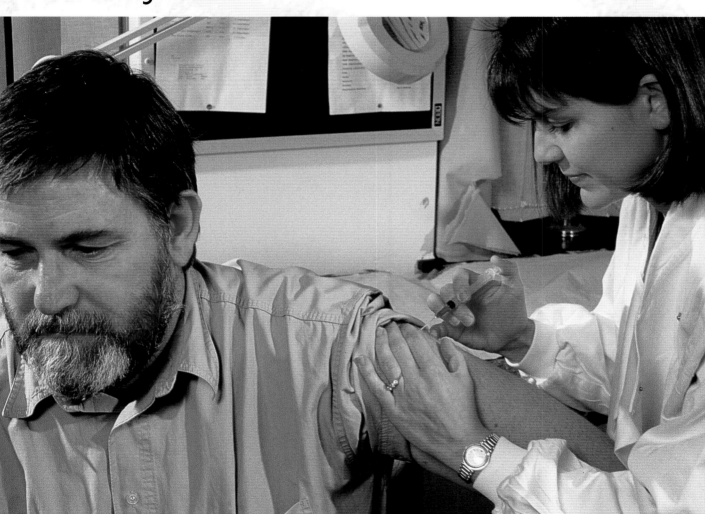

Well and healthy

Colds and **flu** are very common illnesses. Eating plenty of fruit and raw vegetables will help your body to fight these **viruses**.

Washing your hands before eating, getting lots of fresh air and exercise will also help to keep you healthy – and so will plenty of sleep!

Think about it!

If you have a bad **cold**, should you be brave and go to school, or should you stay at home if you can?*

What can you do to stop other people catching your cold?*

*Answers on page 30.

Answers

Page 28

If you have a bad **cold** it is better to stay at home if you can. At school you will probably pass the cold on to your friends. You should always stay at home if you have a **fever**.

Page 29

Cover your nose with a tissue when you sneeze. Used paper hankies are full of **germs**, so do not leave them lying around. Throw them away instead. Cover your mouth with your hand when you cough.

Stay healthy and safe!

1   Always tell an adult if you feel ill or think there is something wrong with you.

2   Never take any **medicine** or use any ointment or lotion unless it is given to you by an adult you trust.

3   Remember, the best way to stay healthy and safe is to eat good food, to drink plenty of water, to keep clean and to wear the correct clothes.

Glossary

blood   red liquid that flows around your body

blood cells   tiny building blocks that form your blood

cold   illness that usually includes a sore throat, runny nose and a cough

fever   when the temperature of your blood becomes hotter than usual

flu   illness, like a cold, that also includes a fever. Flu is short for influenza

germs   tiny living things that can make you ill if they get inside your body

infection   illness caused by germs

infectious   something, especially an illness, that can be passed from one person to another

injection   liquid pushed into the body by a syringe, often to stop you getting an illness

joints   places where two bones meet

lungs   parts of your body that take in oxygen from the air

medicine   substance used to treat or prevent an illness

microscope   something that makes very small things look big enough to see them

mucus   thick liquid made by the body to help wash away germs

muscles   parts of the body that you use to move your bones

painkiller   something which stops you feeling pain

temperature   measure of how hot or cold something is

thermometer   something that measures temperature

throat   part of the body that joins your mouth to the tubes that lead to your lungs and stomach

virus   tiny living things that can make you ill if they get inside your body

Index

Titles in the *It's Catching* series include:

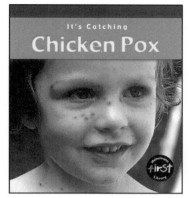

Hardback   0 431 12850 2

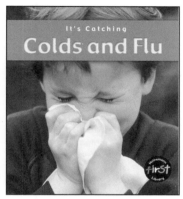

Hardback   0 431 12851 0

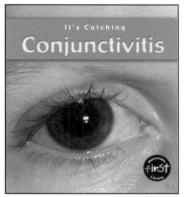

Hardback   0 431 12852 9

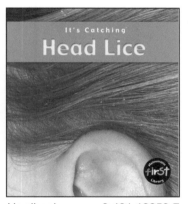

Hardback   0 431 12853 7

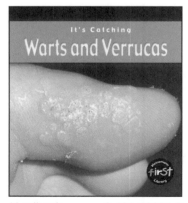

Hardback   0 431 12854 5

Find out about the other titles in this series on our website www.heinemann.co.uk/library